We Are All Terrorists

Some of us are just more terrorizing than others

Nate Zop

tahannaz@gmail.com

We must go after terrorism wherever it threatens free men and women. We can't just stop with a single terrorist or a single terrorist organization; we have to root out the whole system.

—General Colin Powell

Contents

Introduction

THERE HAS NEVER been peace in the world; there is not, and there will never be. One thing we know is that the world is getting less and less safe.

Being born and growing up in one of the poorest countries in the world, I have inherited, along with other children, the economic and political disaster left by colonization and slavery. I grew up looking at people around me with anger and hate because of the terror left by colonization and slavery. The people wanted justice, and since justice was in the hands of the colonizers, they were looking for many options to get revenge. I'm glad that at the time extremist terrorism wasn't that popular. When I moved to the United States a few years ago, like many other immigrants, my dream came true; I was looking forward to embracing the great diversity—the melting pot of America—that

I had studied back in middle school. I quickly discovered that not everything that shines is gold, as I became one of the many victims of stereotyping. Over the years, I found out that this stereotyping targeted certain races, national origins, and religions based on ignorance, racism, greed, injustice, and loneliness. The direct reaction by some victims of this stereotyping can lead them to become radicalized and develop into terrorists. Furthermore, as I started to consider the causes of radicalization and terrorism, I was astonished by my discoveries. From the Ohio State University terrorist attack by Abdul Razak Ali Artan (2016) all the way back to the Columbine High School massacre by Eric Harris and Dylan Klebold (1999), and lately the mass shooting in Las Vegas by Steven Paddock, I came to realize that we all have a seed of terrorism in us and that anyone can become a terrorist. Humans have never been stable beings. A person can change from one minute to the next—and just with a push of button, a pull of a trigger, or a swipe of a machete, chaos can occur. It doesn't matter whether it is called domestic violence, a massacre, domestic terrorism, Islamic extremism, Christian extremism, or gun violence—the truth is that terror will occur, lives may be lost, and communities will be impacted forever. Throughout my many years of investigations, I redefined terrorism and outlined the causes of terrorism, finding few solutions. But the main key to survival is based on the choices we make. But before all, my seven rules for survival are as follows:

- Comply with every safety procedure because it is for your own good.
- Do not go to crowded places unless they are confirmed to be very secure.
- Do not go anywhere alone, especially at night.
- Do not be obsessed with what you can't be or can't have.
- Do not let your anger control you; control it instead.
- Do good and do what is right in the eyes of the people and God.
- Most importantly, *if you see something, say something.*

1
Defining Terrorism

ON DECEMBER 5, 2015, Judge Jeanine Pirro delivered the opening statement of her show *Justice* on the Fox News Channel, following the San Bernardino, California, attack. She said, "Get a gun. Buy one legally. Learn how to shoot. And be primed to use it." Many Americans agreed. But is this the solution? Isn't the person who shoots first the one who has the best chance to hit his or her target? How do you know who is a terrorist and who is not? In fact, we are *all* terrorists, because we can never tell if someone is a terrorist until the worst happens. The person you think you know very well might be the one who will kill you. In today's world, everyone is a suspect, because human beings change their behavior as quickly as chameleons change their color. Two questions remain: What is terrorism, and who can be called a terrorist?

Even today, there is neither an academic nor an accurate legal consensus regarding the definition of terrorism. Some dictionaries define terrorism as "the use of violent acts to frighten people in an area as a way of trying to achieve a political goal." What we know for sure is that terrorism involves fear and terror and, in most cases, ends with death of one or more human beings.

Terrorism comes from the word *terror*, which means extreme fear and horror. For that reason, we can conclude that anything that involves extreme fear or horror is terrorism. But today, when people hear *terrorism*, the image that comes to their minds is a certain religion or people from a certain race. The truth is, terrorism is defined depending on which side you belong to. For many Americans, when they hear *terrorism*, their thoughts are automatically directed to someone with a long beard who is probably Arab and Muslim. But for many people in the Middle East, including the terrorist groups, Americans, Europeans, and everyone who is a partisan of freedom and justice are the terrorists. We should all understand by now that terrorism is diverse and can be found in every race, religion, and country. Arabs were behind the 9/11 attacks, and there is no doubt that they were also Muslims. We can also confirm that before and after 9/11, many terrorist attacks were orchestrated by Arabs and Muslims, but the particularity and the continuity of their attacks

kept out of sight some of the terrorist attacks orchestrated by non-Muslims and non-Arabs. Let's not forget
some of the non-Arab terrorist attacks:

- The Oklahoma bombings, perpetrated by
  Timothy McVeigh (a white US-born Gulf War
  veteran) and Terry Nichols (a white US-born
  farmer and grain-elevator manager) on April
  19, 1995, which left 168 people dead
- The Columbine massacre, led by Dylan Klebold
  and Eric Harris (white US-born high-school students) on April 20, 1999, which left thirteen dead
- The failed shoe bomb attempt on December
  22, 2001, by Richard Reid, a white man of British
  descent
- The Capitol Hill massacre, by Kyle Aaron Huff
  (white, US born) on March 25, 2006, which killed
  six people at a house party
- The Fort Hood, Texas, shooting by Nidal Malik
  Hasan (born in the United States and a US Army
  major) on November 5, 2009, which left thirteen dead
- The shootings by LAPD officer Christopher
  Dorner (black US-born police officer) on February
  3 through 12, 2013, which left four dead
- The Charleston Church shooting by Dylann
  Roof (white, US born) on June 17, 2017, which
  left nine dead

- The Colorado Planned Parenthood shooting by Robert L. Dear (US born) on November 27, 2015, which left three dead
- The Orlando Nightclub shooting by Omar Mateen (US-born citizen) on June 12, 2016, which left forty-nine dead and fifty-three wounded
- The Norway attacks by Anders Behring Breivik (white Norwegian far-right activist) on July 22, 2011, which left seventy-seven dead and more than three hundred casualties
- The Las Vegas concert shooting by Steven Paddock (white US citizen) on October 1, 2017, which left fifty-eight dead and 546 injured

These are just a few examples among many that show how terrorism is spread throughout the world in all colors and all tastes. In addition to that, there is the multitude of violence in families and communities that are turning our world into a cruel battleground.

Terrorism is also defined as "the use of violent acts to frighten the people in an area as a way of trying to achieve a political goal." This definition covers the practices of terrorist groups such as ISIS and Al Qaeda, along with certain nations that are fighting hard to impose their political agenda by using terror. The collision with these groups by Western countries give nightmares to the locals, because the war on terror involves violent acts that frighten innocent people, even though we are also trying to achieve a political goal, which is freedom and democracy. We are fighting for the right cause, but innocent people do pay the price through wars, and in some cases, we may believe that the locals would be better off if they were left in their present living conditions. In fact, we can all confirm now that the people of Libya were better off with Gaddafi. According to Garikai Chengu's article "Libya: From Africa's Richest State Under Gaddafi to Failed State After NATO Intervention," published on October 19, 2015, on the website Global Research, for more than forty years, Gaddafi promoted economic democracy and used nationalized oil wealth to sustain progressive social welfare programs for all Libyans. Under Gaddafi's rule, Libyans enjoyed not only free health care and free education but also free electricity and interest-free loans. But with NATO's intervention, the health-care sector is on the verge of collapse as thousands of Filipino health workers flee the country, institutions of higher education in the eastern part of the country are shut down, and blackouts are a common occurrence in once-thriving Tripoli.

Chengu added that one group that has suffered immensely from NATO's bombing campaign is the nation's women. Unlike many other Arab nations, women in Gaddafi's Libya had the right to education, hold jobs, divorce, hold property, and have an income.

The United Nations Human Rights Council praised Gaddafi for his promotion of women's rights.

When the colonel seized power in 1969, few women went to university. Today, more than half of Libya's university students are women, and one of the first laws Gaddafi passed in 1970 was an equal-pay-for-equal-work law.

Today, however, the new "democratic" Libyan regime is clamping down on women's rights. The new ruling tribes are tied to strongly patriarchal traditions. Also, the chaotic nature of post intervention Libyan politics has given free rein to extremist Islamic forces that see gender equality as a Western perversion.

In 2012, NATO declared that the mission in Libya had been "one of the most successful in NATO history." The truth is, Western interventions have produced nothing but colossal failures in Libya, Iraq, and Syria. Lest we forget, prior to Western military involvement in these three nations, they were the most modern and secular states in the Middle East and North Africa, with the highest regional standards of living and the most advances in women's rights.

Libya is now a refuge for terrorists, and they are now everywhere in the Middle East and on the African continent.

Also, as we look at the situation in Iraq today where ISIS has occupied part of the country, we may be tempted to say that the sacrifices made by the brave men and women during Operation Iraqi Freedom were in vain. One thing is certain: our leaders need to make better choices when it comes to putting those brave soldiers in the fight, because every sacrifice for freedom should not be in vain.

2
Source of Radicalization

TERRORISM IS WITHIN us. Every single day, terrorism is happening in our communities. Terrorism starts from the hate that has dramatically grown in our hearts, but unless it is expressed, people will never know or hear about it. It is important to control our anger when we hate. Anger is the motor of hate, and if it is not controlled, we become monsters, and nothing will stop us. Every heart that is full of hate is like a heart of a terrorist, because it does not know love, kindness, or mercy. Trying to share love with those monsters will not give them compassion toward their potential victims. It will take a lot to heal the heart of a terrorist and will probably take years for a terrorist to become human again; that is why we believe that terrorism will never cease. We will need to learn how to better fight them, but we can also prevent many people from becoming terrorists by sharing love and friendship in our surroundings.

I grew up in one of the poorest countries of the world, which happened to be colonized by France, and most people I encountered had accumulated a lot of hatred toward France and its citizens, because everyone blamed them for enforcing laws that increased poverty and misery. Every kid who went to school and learned about colonization ended up being angry because he or she understood that for centuries, France had been feeding on the country's resources and playing underground games to install leaders who would serve France's interests. As I look back, I see that many of the kids I grew up with could have easily been radicalized and joined a terrorist group, if there had been one, to avenge Africans.

In addition to hate, poverty can influence people in becoming a terrorist. My grandmother used to say that an empty stomach always follows its belly. There is no doubt that terrorist organizations use poverty as an opportunity to recruit. Many reports have shown that most terrorist attacks are executed by poor and uneducated young men and women. Let us not forget the Nigerian group Boko Haram, terrorists whose recruits are mainly youth, and the North Mali terrorist groups that are full of poor little boys and girls who are recruited for a couple of dimes to sacrifice their lives. Many brilliant people of our time have also made a connection between poverty and terrorism and are attempting to shake our generation from its slumber and catalyze global action in the fight against extreme poverty. Among these people are Nobel laureate Archbishop Desmond Tutu, who said, "You can never win a war against terror as long as there are conditions in the world that make people desperate—poverty, disease, ignorance." Former US secretary of state General Colin Powell once stated, "We can't just stop with a single terrorist or a single terrorist organization; we have to go and root out the whole system. We have to go after the whole system."

Ignorance that creates stereotypes and segregation can also lead to terrorism. We need to understand that even a man who assaults his wife or children is a potential terrorist; a racist is a potential terrorist. A person who owns a gun can be labeled as a terrorist for the simple fact that the gun itself can terrorize people or take people's lives. In America, people will not always call it terrorism when a person of the same race, from the same community, shoots and kills dozens of people in a school, a theater, or a park. Unfortunately, this is not just gun violence—it is terrorism. It doesn't matter if the perpetrator is mentally ill or ideologically motivated. Even though we cannot know people very well and what is in their mind, it is important for people in every community to be connected. In today's America, people don't know who their neighbor is, though they live next door to him or her for years—many never try to connect. A simple good morning can start a strong relationship between people who have never met before. One thing we don't realize is that our neighbor might be the one who may assault, rape, or kidnap us or our kids; blow up a train; or kill dozens of people at a nightclub or concert. Individuals, community leaders, religious leaders, and others should put a lot more effort into connecting with their communities. People always come together when tragedies occur, but by that time it is too late. That is why everyone needs to comply with government agencies and laws that are put in place for the safety of all. I was shocked when CNN political commentator and NPR political analyst Angela Rye tried to politicize TSA procedures by comparing them to something a politician said more than ten years ago on a show just because she was treated like everyone else. Ignorance is destroying our modern society. As the scripture says, "my people are destroyed from lack of knowledge" (Hos. 4:6 NIV). As for me and many other noble citizens, we'd rather get our genitals patted down than be blown up in a plane by one of these monsters. With all these crazy things going on, if these procedures didn't exist, I would not step into an airplane, and I'm sure many planes would be coming out of the sky every day. We need to be thankful. Let's not play around with our safety, because terrorists don't care if you are a liberal or a conservative; when an aircraft is down or a bomb explodes, it is a tragedy for all.

Also, since terrorism is mostly associated with Islam in the West, Muslim leaders in Western countries, along with governments, need to find better ways to help every young Muslim to fully integrate in his or her community, because stereotyping can easily facilitate the radicalization of minorities. For example, Abdul Razak Ali Artan, the attacker at Ohio State University in 2016, was described by friends as someone who loved America. They said, "He loved the fact that he had the opportunity to go to school and get a degree." He was described by others as very sweet and a humble person. Prior to his attack, he gave an interview to a campus publication, *The Lantern,* in which he stated, "I wanted to pray in the open, but I was kind of scared with everything going on in the media. I'm a Muslim; it's not what the media portrays me to be. If people look at me, a Muslim praying, I don't know what they're going to think. But I don't blame them. It's the media that put that picture in their heads, so they're just going to have it, and it's going to make them feel uncomfortable. I was kind of scared right now. But I just did it. I relied on God. I went over to the corner and just prayed." Artan, who was a sweet and humble man, suddenly turned into a bitter and angry person just because he couldn't fit in his new community. Stereotyping and segregation probably played a big role in his radicalization. But he also mentioned the media, which he thought made people think a certain way, and that raises the question of whether the media sees the consequences of its reports. The media can be a big weapon of destruction if news organizations don't report accurate information. They also need to provide guidance and clarification about their reports.

3
Islam and Terrorism

CONSPIRACY THEORIES ARE not always true, but sometimes things make sense in theory more than what we are being told. Are we winning the much-publicized war on terror? Terrorism increased when the war on terror started. Based on the analysis of CNN anchor Fareed Zakaria in his documentary "War on ISIS," prior to 2001, the declaration of war on terrorism, there had not been even one terrorist attack on Iraqi soil or in Afghanistan. When I was growing up, snakes were the only things that made us unsafe, but today, everywhere I go I do not trust the other person walking beside me. In fact, every day, I walk out of my house feeling like I'm a martyr because I do not know if I will make it back home safe. Nowadays, people are afraid of Arabs and Muslims, even though most of them have never come across one of them. The truth is, everybody is a potential terrorist—it doesn't matter if a person is Muslim, Arab, Caucasian, black, Chinese, or any other group.

Terrorism should not be attributed to a religion or a certain race; terrorism comes from within. So why is publicized terrorism attributed to Arabs or Muslims? In fact, most of the spectacular terrorist attacks that have happened during my lifetime have been done by Muslims or people who claim to be Muslim. All religions, including Islam, Christianity, Judaism, and Buddhism, claim to be peaceful. We cannot deny that in every religion, there have been certain times when some type of terrorism was involved. We cannot ignore the Christian crusades that killed thousands, nor can we ignore the massacres during the multiple Muslim conquests during the reign of the prophet. Sometimes, when we look at terrorism involving people who claim to be Muslims, we can quickly understand that at a certain level, they are interpreting some scripture from the Quran even though they may interpret it differently from most people. In fact, that kind of terrorism is similar to the Colorado Springs Planned Parenthood shooting by Robert Lewis Dear Jr., which left two civilians and one police officer dead. He did claim to be antiabortion based on his religious beliefs and wanted to defend his "religion" and babies, calling himself "a warrior for the babies." He is not in any way different from the Islamic extremists. Islamic extremists seem to be living in a certain era of human history, but sometimes some Muslim reactions to terrorist attacks do not help the issue. I think Muslims must be the first to condemn each terrorist attack from Islamic extremists, and Islamic countries need to take the lead in fighting extremist terrorism. Also, if we believe that the Quran is authentic and everything that we read inside is true, then Islamic extremists may be literally following what is written even though every shiny thing may not be gold. For example, the Quran holds some stories that are found in the Old Testament of the Bible, and if we want to refer just to the "eye for an eye" law, the law of retaliation that is in both the Quran and the Bible, this law never brings peace in any society but is used legally by some Islamic governments and in territories controlled by Islamist terrorists. If Jesus had never come to earth, Christians would be using that same law, but Jesus gave a more peaceful addition to it when he said, in Matthew 5:38–42 (NIV), "You have heard that it was said, 'Eye for eye, and tooth for tooth.' But I tell you, do not resist an evil person. If anyone slaps you on the right cheek, turn to them the other cheek also. And if anyone wants to sue you and take your shirt, hand over your coat as well. If anyone forces you to go one mile, go with them two miles. Give to the one who asks you, and do not turn away from the one who wants to borrow from you." This passage has helped me personally to refrain from retaliation, because retaliation only brings more retaliations. It is important for every religion to recognize its responsibility in terrorism. A Muslim friend told me once that once a person kills, he or she is no longer Muslim, even if he or she was praying in a mosque prior to the crime. Many Muslims share this view, and that does not help defeat extremist terrorism. No religion is perfect, and anyone who embraces a religion prior to committing a crime carries that religion with him or her. Recognizing the origins of an issue always helps resolve it; therefore, the members of every religion that is said to breed extremist terrorism should take responsibility by reviewing their teachings and methods and providing more updates and training to their leaders.

4
Comparing the Scriptures

EVERY LIFE MATTERS and everyone who takes or tries to take a human life in the name of any ideology or religion is a terrorist and should be punished by the court of law. Many holy scriptures could lead to radicalization. The difference is how those scriptures are received. The way the message is taught has a great impact on its receiver. Based on personal experience, many people use verses out of their normal context, sometimes for their own benefit, and that can change the scriptures' meaning entirely. That possibility exists in all religions, but there is a myth behind the Quran. I have been told numerous times by Muslims that the Quran should not be translated and that every available translation is inaccurate. The question that has

always been in my mind is how will people understand their religion if they can't read their holy book?
More than 70 percent of Muslims do not speak or read
Arabic. It comes back to teaching, and since we are all
human, every teacher can use any passage and teach it
the way he or she feels it. When it comes to the Bible, it
is well translated into many languages, and everybody
can have access to it. This, too, has been criticized by
Muslims, who say that the Bible is not accurate. Even
though it is well translated, many Christians twist the
Bible for their own benefits, and that has hurt the
credibility of pastors worldwide. The difference is
many people use the scriptures for fraud or to gather
wealth, but for the most part, the translated Bible,
which has two parts—the Old and New Testament—
gives a clear understanding of what a Christian should
do. The Old Testament is full of stories related to
the people of Israel, their interaction with God, their
failures, their battles, and their victories. The New
Testament starts with the coming of Jesus, his minis-
tries, his death, his resurrection, and his coming again.
For centuries, Christians and Muslims have fought
to prove which religion is "good," but this is a battle
that can never be won. It is a spiritual war, and everyone needs to be praying hard instead of killing each
other. A lot of work needs to be done to bring peace
between human beings. Religions are supposed to
heal, not wound people. I have read all the holy books,

and what I found is that unlike the Old Testament and the Quran, the New Testament does not have any message that tends to be violent, and since Christians say that the New Testament is the completion of the Old Testament, it appears to clear most violent passages of the Old Testament claimed by Muslims. Here are some verses of the New Tetaments.

> Beloved, never avenge yourselves, but leave it to the wrath of God, for it is written, "Vengeance is mine, I will repay, says the Lord." To the contrary, "if your enemy is hungry, feed him; if he is thirsty, give him something to drink; for by so doing you will heap burning coals on his head." Do not be overcome by evil, but overcome evil with good. (Rom. 12:19–21)

> Then they will deliver you up to tribulation and put you to death, and you will be hated by all nations for my name's sake. And then many will fall away and betray one another and hate one another. And many false prophets will arise and lead many astray. And because lawlessness will be increased, the love of many will grow cold. But the one who endures to the end will be saved. (Matt. 24:9–13)

Turn away from evil and do good; seek peace and pursue it. (Ps. 34:14)

But I say to you, love your enemies and pray for those who persecute you, so that you may be sons of your Father who is in heaven. For he makes his sun rise on the evil and on the good, and sends rain on the just and on the unjust. For if you love those who love you, what reward do you have? Do not even the tax collectors do the same? And if you greet only your brothers, what more are you doing than others? Do not even the Gentiles do the same? You therefore must be perfect, as your heavenly Father is perfect. (Matt. 5:44–48)

You have heard that it was said, "An eye for an eye and a tooth for a tooth." But I say to you, do not resist the one who is evil. But if anyone slaps you on the right cheek, turn to him the other also. (Matt. 5:38–39)

Let every person be subject to the governing authorities. For there is no authority except from God, and those that exist have been instituted by God. Therefore, whoever resists the authorities resists what God has appointed, and those who resist will incur judgment. For rulers are not a terror to good conduct, but too bad. Would you have no fear of the one who is in authority? Then do what is good, and you will receive his approval, for he is God's servant for your good. But if you do wrong, be afraid, for he does not bear the sword in vain. For he is the servant of God, an avenger who carries out God's wrath on the wrongdoer. Therefore, one must be in subjection, not only to avoid God's wrath but also for the sake of conscience. (Rom. 13:1–5)

After reading these verses, I said to myself, *I wish the Quran also had a kind of "New Testament."* The following are verses that Christians and Muslims use to accuse each other of having a violent religion.

Here are verses from the Old Testament:

That is not true. But a man of the hill country of Ephraim, called Sheba the son of Bichri, has lifted his hand against King David; give up him alone, and I will withdraw from the city." And the woman said to Joab, "Behold, his head shall be thrown to you over the wall." Then the woman went to all the people in her wisdom. And they cut off the head of Sheba the son of Bichri, and threw it out to Joab. (2 Sam. 20:21)

When the LORD your God brings you into the land where you are entering to possess it, and clears away many nations before you, the Hittites and the Girgashites and the Amorites and the Canaanites and the Perizzites and the Hivites and the Jebusites, seven nations greater and stronger than you. And when the LORD your God delivers them before you and you defeat them, then you shall destroy them. You shall make no covenant with them and show no favor to them. (Deut. 7:1–2)

The Lord our God delivered him over to us and we struck him down, together with his sons and his whole army. At that time, we took all his towns and destroyed them— men, women and children. We left no sur- vivors. But the livestock and the plunder from the towns we had captured we carried off for ourselves. From Aroer on the rim of the Arnon Gorge, and from the town in the gorge, even as far as Gilead, not one town was too strong for us. (Deut. 2:33–36)

Joshua said to the people of Israel, "The Lord has given you the city of the all silver, and gold, and vessels of brass and iron, are consecrated unto the Lord: They shall come into the treasury of the Lord. The people destroyed all that was in the city, both man and woman, young and old, and ox and sheep, and ass, with the edge of the sword. (Josh. 6:21–23)

Here are some verses from the Quran:

As to those who reject faith, I will punish them with terrible agony in this world and in the Hereafter, nor will they have anyone to help. (Quran 3:56)

Soon shall We cast terror into the hearts of the Unbelievers, for that they joined companions with Allah, for which He had sent no authority. (Quran 3:151)

So, let those who fight in the cause of Allah who sell the life of this world for the Hereafter. And he who fights in the cause of Allah and is killed or achieves victory - We will bestow upon him a great reward. (Quran 4:74)

Those who believe fight in the cause of Allah... (Quran 4:76)

They but wish that ye should reject Faith, as they do, and thus be on the same footing (as they): But take not friends from their ranks until they flee in the way of Allah (From what is forbidden). But if they turn renegades, seize them and slay them wherever ye find them; and (in any case) take no friends or helpers from their ranks. (Quran 4:89)

The punishment of those who wage war against Allah and His messenger and strive to make mischief in the land is only this, that they should be murdered or crucified or their hands and their feet should be cut off on opposite sides or they should be imprisoned; this shall be as a disgrace for them in this world, and in the hereafter, they shall have a grievous chastisement. (Quran 5:33)

I will cast terror into the hearts of those who disbelieve. Therefore, strike off their heads and strike off every fingertip of them. (Quran 8:12)

> And fight with them until there is no more
> fitna (disorder, unbelief) and religion is all
> for Allah. (Quran 8:39)

Religion is a way of life for many human beings and is the foundation of educating kids in millions of families across the globe. When people see that their way of life is not respected, they feel like they should act, and the only way for people to defend it or make people respect it is through terror. Terrorists use death to intimidate people because death is feared by all. The world is perverted to the point that people do not know what is good and bad anymore. In America, many people would try to avenge their religion if they could. For Christians, it is a sin to watch pornographic movies, but when you watch one and see a woman or man doing those sinful actions while wearing a crucifix around his or her neck, you should be furious, even if you were enjoying the movie, because as a Christian, your most precious symbol, the reason of your existence, is being disrespected. This can be compared to the feeling you get when the flag of your country is burned or disrespected, because the flag is an important symbol of a country. Today, many Christians are so silent that they are being transformed into nonbelievers. For many Christians, Christianity is only for comfort, and so they make sure they are giving much to the church so that when they die they have a good funeral. Certainly, Americans have learned many ways to protest, and those ways are very peaceful, such as voting for the laws they believe in and protesting in the street to get their voice heard. No one can defend a God. If you think your religion is that great and powerful, you should let your God defend himself. How will killing people persuade others to follow your religion? Instead of killing innocents, live by example. Make people see something special about you, and they may endorse your way of life.

5
Lesson from a Believer

MY GRANDFATHER HAD a great impact on my family and myself. Because of him, we have experienced most of the big religions in the world. In fact, my grandfather was born an atheist, became a Muslim, and ended up being Christian until his death. My grandfather, whose name was Peter, was the leader of our tribe. He had a traditional name, *Suana,* which means "beans." He grew up as an atheist and took advantage of the benefits that came with that upbringing. He told us that he used to possess a lot of power based on witchcraft. With that spiritual power, he could make people die without a gun, a machete, or any physical touch. With that power, he could capture people's souls and send them to hell. In the West, people might not know about this—even our young generation does not—but people like my grandfather could tell someone that he or she will die the next day, and the next day will be that person's funeral, though he or she was very healthy the day before. It was impossible to steal from my grandfather, because when you took something from him, you wouldn't be able to move from there or put it back; you would be wandering around there until he arrived to catch you. My dad and my uncles confirmed with me that at night, there were lights in the sky. People today call them UFOs, but in fact these were people flying by night and fighting in the sky, town against town every night. My grandfather stuck in that life until he found Islam. He converted to Islam because in his heart he was convinced that Islam was way better than the life he was living and that Islam had principles of respecting one another and preserving human life. All the family converted to Islam, and since my grandfather ended up with six wives and thirty-six children, plus his brothers, they were a big addition to the Muslim community. As a chief, he used his leadership to expand Islam to neighboring towns and villages. It was in his walk with Islam that he found Jesus. He became Christian after working for a couple of years with missionaries, and still today in the country of Burkina Faso, many Muslims still work with or for missionaries. My grandfather described his relationship with Canadian missionaries as friendly and respectful. Over the years, the only difference he saw between the Muslim faith and the Christian faith was that Christian scripture guaranteed salvation, as opposed to Islam, which required certain efforts to get to heaven. And knowing that human beings are never perfect, my grandfather believed that Christianity made more sense. Even with little knowledge of the Bible, he started preaching the gospel to the people to whom he had previously preached Islam. During one of his rallies, he preached to people, and they were so happy that they gave him a wife, and as a "baby Christian," he took the wife. That was his sixth and last wife. For a long period in part of Africa, when you did something good to a community, they would give you a wife to create strong ties between you and them forever.

My grandfather grew in his faith and died as Christian in 2004 after a century on earth. He had been blessed with dozens of grandchildren, including me. His experience with religions was a rich heritage for me in addition to the life I have lived surrounded by Muslims, because some of my uncles and cousins are still Muslims. Throughout my childhood, I saw the net difference in education between my Muslim relatives and myself. When I look back at some of those days with my Muslim cousins, I can clearly confirm that poor education could be a key factor in radicalization. I did notice that most of the kids who were

violent in their habits were born to poor and uneducated parents who had just some few notions of Islam;
the only things they knew were told by the imam of
the village, who himself barely held much knowledge
of the Quran. It is like my grandfather taking a sixth
wife even though he was a Christian—as I previously
said, a "baby Christian." My Muslim cousins and friends
labeled us Christians as nonbelievers, eaters of dead
animals. Some few radicals will not eat the meat of
animals that are slaughtered by Christians, and they
will not eat with Christians. But generally, in Burkina
Faso where I am from, it is very common to see two sib-
lings of different faiths. After my grandfather became
Christian, his brother refused to become a Christian
and remained Muslim until his death, but he did not
stop some of his children from becoming Christian.
Still, today, during Christmas, Christians share food
with Muslim neighbors and friends. They make sure
that we don't slaughter pigs, because Muslims don't
eat pork. During Ramadan and Tabaski, Muslims share
food with Christians.

6
Education is the Key

EDUCATION PLAYS AN important role in every human life. Since religion is the foundation of their education for many people, it can be deadly if children do not get the right information when growing up. That is why guns, tanks, and fighter jets alone cannot win over terrorism, because unless you wipe every single person that you think might be a terrorist from the earth, even the little brain that will escape will keep the ideology alive. In fact, the war on terror seemed to make things worse, as it spread the ideology beyond borders through the news media. The method that was used to fight Islamic terrorism was working. Ideology is the answer to ideology. The school system that is spreading across the globe, teaching the virtues of liberty and justice, was winning over the extremist ideology. That is one of the reasons why Boko Haram in Nigeria is attacking schools—because they found out that they were losing as children grew up being well taught about freedom and justice. My personal experience shows that it is hard to brainwash someone who grew up with certain values, such as freedom, liberty, and knowledge of one's rights and duties. For example, even today, many people around the world, whether they are Muslim or Christian, are giving everything they can to come to the United States. It is impossible to convince them that life is tough in the United States and that they will be exposed to many struggles once they get there. The only reason they insist so much in getting to America is because since they were kids, they have been taught how beautiful and powerful America is. Through school and television, they learned about the American way of life, which is solely based on freedom, justice, and free enterprise, and that kept them dreaming and praying to the good Lord for opportunities to get there. Many people outside of the United States know more about the United States than most Americans. People love and support the United States more when they are outside than when they are inside. It is important for Americans to embrace intelligence over ignorance. Even though America has the best technology and information tools, Americans are among the least informed people of the world. When I was in college, many students used to ask me questions that were very disturbing.

Back in Africa, we used to think that Americans were supersmart, but when I came to the United States, I couldn't believe that a college student could be holding a smartphone in his or her hands and yet believe that people ride lions to school in Africa. One of my classmates was angry when the teacher let me present a PowerPoint about Africa, because he said he didn't care about any other nation since the United States was the greatest nation. I couldn't disagree with him, but I did tell him that the only way you can defeat your enemies and stay strong is by knowing them and staying up-to-date with the world.

7

Is Abortion Equal to Terrorism?

TERRORISM IS NOT only the mass killings that are executed by extremists; it is any act of terror that takes a human life. I found it a little hypocritical when one of my favorite presidents, Barack Obama, shed tears for gun control while he and the Democrats have no feeling for the small ones. Supporting mass abortion is terrorism. Every life matters, and those little angels deserve to live as every other human. In fact, the babies we kill might be the ones who would have become doctors or scientists to find cures for cancer or other diseases or perhaps find the secret to longevity for those who believe in immortality. For people who justify abortion because of rape, incest, or the mother's life in danger, it is important to understand that if abortion was only performed in these cases, not many would oppose it. However, the majority of abortions are from unplanned pregnancy (Guttmacher Institute), but there are many ways available to prevent unplanned pregnancies and even procedures for early termination before the first heartbeat. I think it is important to put more effort on preventing rather than encouraging abortion. For people who say that men should not tell women what to do with their bodies, they need to be reminded that no one owns themselves once they are citizens of a country. Every citizen is an asset of his or her country—that is why if any of them are taken into captivity, some brave citizens who were fortunate not to be aborted by their mothers will risk their lives to rescue them. Once a woman is pregnant, the unborn baby does not belong to her anymore; it belongs to the country. That is why the government put resources in places for single mothers and welfare. There are also a lot of adoption agencies and lovely families always available to welcome those angels. If the government does not put some regulations on abortion, there will be chaos. Who are we to decide the fate of another human? If we are that responsible, we need to start by preventing pregnancy. It is very rare to see women die because of pregnancy, so why do these little angels have to get their right to life taken away from them? Every life, even unborn ones, should be protected.

Abortion can also affect the mother and even take her life in the process. I still have bad memories of the consequences of the abortion that took the life of my junior-high-school girlfriend. Her name was Adel; she was a sweetheart and a very beautiful girl. I remember we used to hold hands and walk along the road to her home, and we promised to each other that wherever life took us, we would never cut the strong ties we had made over the school year. After graduation, I moved to the United States, and the distance was too far to keep the flame alive. She met a teenager and engaged in a love relationship. Every time we had a chance to talk on the phone, Adel was honest with me, and our friendship was strong. They were both sixteen. Since they were very young and since it is common for teenagers to make mistakes, they made one. She became pregnant, and with the stress and pressure of the community on her, she made the wrong choice, which was to get rid of it. In fact, in areas such as Africa and even in some very conservative places in the United States, being pregnant as a teenager is seen as disgraceful. Her family decided to find a good doctor who performed abortion. It did go well, but after the abortion, she had some infections and died of complications. When I heard the news, I was more than sad, as she could have lived healthy with a baby who would be healthy and would strongly contribute to humanity. As Martin Luther King Jr. once said, "The Negro cannot win if he is willing to sacrifice the lives of his children for comfort and safety. How can the 'Dream' survive if we murder the children? Every aborted baby is like a slave in the womb of his or her mother. The mother decides his or her fate."

My grandmother always tells me that a person who eats an egg has eaten a chicken, because it is an egg that becomes a chicken, which simply correlates to the fact that every aborted embryo is a human, and whoever killed it or supported that killing is also a killer. Abortion is against the law of nature and the survival of the human race, and everyone who supports it should be called a terrorist. In a country like the United States, with great resources in medical technology, where most pregnancies can be protected and secured to birth, women should be encouraged to keep the future leaders and contributors of keeping America great, instead of disposing of valuable citizens. People are accusing Hispanics of having many kids and taking tax money to feed their kids, and they forget that it is because abortion is not common in their culture that they are having a lot of babies. Statistics show that the white and black population are decreasing over the years relative to Hispanics. According to 2010 census data, African Americans make up 12.6 percent of the US population, but the Centers for Disease Control (CDC) reports that African American women accounted for 35.4 percent of all abortions in

2009. The Guttmacher Institute (AGI) puts that percentage at 30 percent. Their most recent numbers were from 2008. Similarly, AGI tells us that Hispanic women accounted for 25 percent of US abortions in 2008, although Hispanics make up just 16.3 percent of the US population. The CDC lists the percentage of Hispanic abortions at 20.6 percent. Compare those numbers to non-Hispanic whites, who make up 63.7 percent of America's population but account for 36 percent of all US abortions (37.7 percent according to the CDC). Every day in America, an average of 3,315 human beings lose their lives to abortion.

Based on these percentages, between 683 and 829 of those babies are Hispanic, between 1,193 and 1,174 are white, and between 995 and 1,207 are African American. With the implantation of Planned Parenthood in minority neighborhoods, not only are poor people's children being killed at a far greater percentage than rich people's children, it's possible they're being killed in greater numbers. Isn't that terrorism? With some people describing the goal of Planned Parenthood as targeting minorities, when we look at the statistics, even though the white population in the United States outnumbers the African American population five to one, abortion may well be killing more black children each day than white children. John Piper, a white pastor with a heart for racial justice, remarks on the disparity of abortion this way:

The de facto effect (I don't call it the main cause, but net effect) of putting abortion clinics in the urban centers is that the abortion of Hispanic and black babies is more than double their percentage of the population. Every day 1,300 black babies are killed in America. Seven hundred Hispanic babies die every day from abortion. Call this what you will—when the slaughter has an ethnic face and the percentages are double that of the white community and the killers are almost all white, something is going on here that ought to make the lovers of racial equality and racial harmony wake up.

How many people die of extremist terrorism every year? In 2014, 32,658 people were killed due to terrorism around the world. In January 2014, the Guttmacher Institute reported that 1.05 million abortions were performed in the United States in 2012, and 4.8 percent of these occurred between week sixteen and thirty-two of pregnancy, meaning that 4.8 percent were live babies. How are we different from terrorists if we even kill more than what they kill? Do we need the media to start showing live coverage of abortions for us to feel angry or protest it? A live scene of an abortion and the images of those fetuses on the news will bring more fear and sadness than what we see every day about extremists.

8
Guns and Terrorism

THE ATROCITIES COMMITTED by extremists that the media shows us are no different from abortions. They frighten people—maybe because they involve weapons such as knives (beheading), guns, and explosives. Previously, I mentioned that a person who carries a gun might be a terrorist because anyone who doesn't have a gun will be terrorized by just knowing that his or her neighbor owns one. There is more than just owning a gun—supporting gun policies could also mean involuntarily supporting the big network of terrorists, and that is the same for those who do nothing about it. As Napoleon Bonaparte said, "The world suffers a lot. Not because the violence of bad people but because of the silence of the good people." We are all guilty if we don't do anything about the flow of guns throughout the world. I used to drive around farms in

Nebraska. I met a lot of farmers, and I remember that the father of one of my coworkers owned about sixty-seven guns, along with a lot of explosives. I was certain that he was just collecting them and he was probably going to use one of those guns once or twice a year to shoot a deer or wild turkeys. His son also had fourteen guns. A person like Berry, with his many collected guns and explosives, will never refuse to do a background check or register his guns if he can get any gun he needs. It is important to know who handles guns and which guns are handled, because the flow of guns is falling into the hands of criminals and extremists. A report from the US Government Accountability Office in 2015 states that more than seventy thousand guns recovered from crime scenes in Mexico between 2009 and 2014 could be traced back to the United States. That represents 70 percent of all crime guns recovered and traced in Mexico during that period.

The report underscores the extent to which American firearms are a contributor not just to crime in the United States but also to violence that happens south of the border. Half of the seized weapons were long guns—shotguns or rifles. "According to Mexican government officials, high caliber rifles are the preferred weapon used by drug trafficking organizations," the report found. Those rifles include the assault-style weapons that have lately been used in mass shootings in the United States.

The flow of guns from the United States to Mexico shares some DNA with the black-market drug trade between the two countries. "Firearms that criminal organizations acquire from the United States are primarily transported overland into Mexico using the same routes and methods employed when smuggling bulk cash south and drugs north across the US-Mexico border," the report notes.

The report also says that criminal organizations in Mexico rely on straw purchases in the United States to acquire guns legally and then funnel them southward. "Firearm trafficking organizations also frequently obtain firearms from unlicensed private sellers in secondary markets, particularly at gun shows and flea markets or through classified ads or private-party Internet postings." This report is one out of many that is showing that the uncontrolled gun flow is taking many lives around us, in our communities, schools, and our world.

We all agree that anywhere guns are involved, death or destruction may occur. The misuse of guns doesn't only affect others; it can have a disastrous impact on one's life. Every time that I get a chance to look at the bloody left eye of my dad, it makes me feel nervous as I remember the scene my mom described to me years ago. In fact, my dad almost lost his left eye years ago. Back in the 1970s, when guns were still operating mostly under gunpowder, many people, including my dad, loved guns and used to hunt deer, wild turkeys, guinea fowl, partridge, wild chicken, rabbits, hippopotamus, and antelopes. Unlike today, there were still a lot of wild animals around, as it was common to see a deer or a rabbit one hundred feet from the house. One day, my dad walked out of the house holding his gun and suddenly spotted some partridges in the neighbor's yard. He charged the gun, aimed at them, and fired a shot. My dad had been using this same gun for years; he knew it very well. But he couldn't imagine that the outcome of this shot would be so different from what he was used to. When he fired that gun, the gun did what it was supposed to, but a second explosion occurred, and that explosion blew up the gun and spread burning gunpowder all over my dad's face. He dropped the gun and fell to the ground. He had killed two partridges, but he was lying there fighting for his life. My mom, who heard the unusual explosion, ran out of the house and discovered the unthinkable. She saw my dad lying there covered with blood and barely moving. She was flooded by tears and called for help. My uncles showed up and took my dad on a motorbike to the hospital, which was forty miles away. Luckily, he was treated and came out of it alive, though his eye will remain red the rest of his life. Every year, around the time of the incident, he experiences a lot of pain in his eyes, and he always goes to the doctor to make sure nothing else can further affect his eyes. Even though my dad went through all this, it did not stop him from using guns. He still goes hunting and still loves guns, and that is a perfect example of gun lovers who will never give away their guns for any reason.

In the United States, people refer to the Second Amendment to the Constitution, which states that "a well-regulated militia, being necessary to the security of a free state, the right of the people to keep and bear arms, shall not be infringed." This amendment enables private gun ownership in the United States. Despite current gun regulations, firearms can be bought at gun shows or privately from unlicensed dealers with no background checks. People report that they need them for safety and/or sport. However, having a firearm in the home increases the rate of suicide, homicide, domestic violence, and accidents. The presumed security is questioned, especially since owner and family suicide vastly outnumbers self-protective events. Gun-related suicide in America accounts for most violent death occurrences. This high suicide rate is shockingly underappreciated. According to a review published online in February 2010 by Steven Lippmann, MD, guns have a negative impact on communities. In 2005, out of a total of 541 firearm-related deaths in Kentucky, 375 were gunshot suicides (69 percent), homicides accounted for 143, accidents claimed 11, 9 died in police shootings, and 3 fatalities were unspecified. During 2006 and 2007, again, approximately 70 percent of gunshot deaths were suicides.

Most Americans are unaware that gunshot suicide occurs much more often than all other shooting deaths combined. Suicide by gunfire is the fastest-growing and most common means of suicide, regardless of age, gender, race, or educational level. It is the leading cause of death in those who purchase firearms for the first time. Despite the fact that guns are generally obtained for personal security, 83 percent of gun fatalities in a home are suicide. Among 395 shooting deaths in Seattle during one year, 333 were by suicide, 41 were domestic violence incidents, 12 were accidents, and only 9 involved an intruder. Women commit suicide three times as often when firearms are present in a home than in domiciles without them. Despite mental illness being an important factor, most suicide attempts are impulsive and done under stress, when upset and/or intoxicated, but without psychopathology. Awareness about the frequency of such unplanned acts is limited. Having firearms readily available increases the lethality of such impulsivity.

Guns are the most frequently used means involved in deaths by domestic violence, increasing the rate of killing an intimate partner. Five times as many women are shot to death in homes where such weaponry is available in contrast to households without them. Family-member homicide is much more likely than stopping a trespasser. Sadly, many American children are shot to death every day.

Gun violence has a negative impact on society. Beyond death and disability, survivors of a shooting endure psychological trauma and grief. Violence-exposed children experience developmental consequences, and adults also evidence personal compromise. Living in communities where fear of getting shot is common has detrimental effects on people and teaches inappropriate role modeling about responsible behavior to future generations.

A visit to hospitals, trauma centers, and rehabilitation or nursing home facilities will reveal how flooded they are with victims of shootings.

Every day, when we see images of thousands of children affected by wars in Africa, we hear about child soldiers, and we are heartbroken, but we don't realize that our support for certain laws or even our silence about the use of weapons is creating the chaos.

It is impossible to talk about wars without mentioning guns and weapons. If what is happening in Africa now is not terrorism, what else can we call it? Many people from the West are taking advantage of that chaos to expand their wealth. It looks like the Cold War has been deported to Africa, as most wars involve countries from the West on both sides of the conflicts.

9
Was Colonization Terrorism?

THE FIRST AND foremost terrorism on the African continent was colonization. Colonization should be qualified as terrorism. It has been implemented in Africa and is still being used to create chaos there. Before European colonization, Africa was much more peaceful than what it is today. Colonization has turned Africans to monsters. It is evident that terrorism origi- nates from the Western colonial powers, but none would dare to concede this for fear of retaliation. When the European businessmen explored new world markets for diminishing resources and their armed forces invaded and occupied the vast Islamic world and African lands, there was no television, Internet, video cameras, and stone-throwing public—no voices of reason to call them foreign mercenaries, aggressors, and terrorists. The colonization scheme of things was not an outcome of Western democratic values to spread freedom, liberty, and justice but ferocity of violence and killings of millions and millions of human lives for the empires to be built on colored bloodbaths. Nobody wants to think of it or even apologize for all those children who died under the gunpowder and the oppression of colonization. In addition to that, Africa still suffers from the wounds and the emptiness left by slavery. Africa is still being exploited and terrorized daily. Slavery took all man power of Africa across the oceans and fed some of it to the sea. The ones that survived were later named black Americans. Like many Africans, I used to think that black Americans were lazy, violent thieves, because of what I was seeing on television back in Africa, but I found out that I was wrong when I became one. Most black Americans are still technically under slavery, because there are no opportunities for them to succeed. In fact, let's look back to the end of slavery. My grandfather told me that slavery ended because of the progress of technology. In fact, America has reached its dream of food sustainability and has had the ability to produce more than enough food, and since slaves were mainly used in agriculture, it was easy for America to use a different tool to extend its leadership in the world. My grandfather was right; laws and declarations ended slavery, but no good politics were put in place to reha-bilitate these poor Africans. In fact, neither they nor their children could ever dream of owning a piece of the ground they died farming. The only thing they did was to transform the slave to an entertainer—in other words, transform the ancient slave to a modern slave. Schools, which were now available to slaves, enforced different strategies. How can a child of a slave pretend to take loans to school if he is not even guaranteed of getting a job that will allow him to pay that loan back? Now, even in the twenty-first century, things are get-ting worse as companies with good-paying jobs will not hire black people for what they are worth. I have been a victim of it, and many friends have experienced a lot of rejections simply because of their skin color. In this world now, all races are viewed more favorably than black people. That is a reason why many black Americans keep serving their master by selling drugs to their people and being looked at as the devil. And their daughters are the ones behind the booming hotel businesses with most of them involved in prostitution.

Many Africans fought very hard against terrorist attacks from Europeans for years because they didn't want slavery and the stealing of African resources to happen. This is not different from today's terror-ism, and it was even worse than the Holocaust; yet everyone feels compassionate when Nazi atrocities are mentioned, while no one ever points out the real terrorism behind the chaos involving African slaves. One white friend told me that black people have the same chances white people have in America, and I asked him, "If your great-grandparents were slaves, your granddad spent most of his life in jail because he is black, and your dad is still in jail because he had to take care of himself since he was eleven years old, what chances would you have?" I challenge you to look at all the kids adopted by white families; 90 percent will become successful in life. It's always easy to sit and blame.

10
A Letter to the Motherland

WITH THE EXTREMIST terrorism taking over the world and now invading Africa, which is already full of problems, the hope for a prosperous and developed Africa is in jeopardy. One day, while walking around Central Park in New York City, I saw a man in his late sixties who appeared to need help. He was sitting by the bus stop and trying to get up. He was struggling, so I walked toward him and grabbed his hand to help him up.

And he asked me, "Where are you from?"

I replied, "Africa."

"Where in Africa?"

"Burkina Faso," I said.

"Good. My name is Madou Keita, from Mali. I have visited Burkina Faso and many countries in Africa. I came to the United States twenty years ago, and I have never been back home. I have a daughter who is eighteen, and she just started to file adjustment of status for me, because for my entire time here, I didn't get a chance to be legal. Lately, I heard the north of my country, Mali, has been taken over by terrorists, and I think that will worsen the living conditions of people there. Do you have an hour?"

"Yes," I replied.

And he said, "I would like to write a letter for you as a souvenir, and I hope you will share it with your friends and the coming generation."

Here is his letter:

> Grandson, I'm writing this letter in an easy English, French, and any other languages that you may speak so that after you read it you will think twice before making the next move in your life. A couple of years ago, I left my country for a better life here. I fled because of poverty, hunger, and diseases. Today, I heard it has become worse, as extremist terrorism is creating chaos everywhere so listen carefully.
>
> Every day, I spend my time in a basement of a building, washing dishes in a restaurant somewhere in America, along with some Mexicans. We are being treated very well,

like every modern-day slave. I'm not complaining about the situation in which I'm living, but I'm certainly trying to make you understand that I could have gotten a better offer with a bachelor's degree. There are probably many reasons why I'm stuck here, and one of the reasons—the major one—is because I do not have the proper paperwork to get a better job; there is no other alternative. After all, I came here just to pay the thousands of dollars to go to school and learn something that I can't even use. Who should I blame? My country, my family (who invested all the family funds on me hoping for a better future), or should I blame Africa? I came to realize that the America I saw from outside is totally different from the one I'm in now. Even though Mom and Dad put all their savings onto me, I heard that they haven't changed their habits, as every evening they sit in front of our lovely mud house with the same smile, thinking of me and wishing the best for me, even though my brothers and sisters are left hopeless. I remember that we used to go to the farm every morning. We came back home in the evening and after eating super went to my aunt Habibou's hut for two or three stories before going to bed. Unlike the statistics that suggest that people don't live longer in Africa, my aunt was in the sixties younger than my grandmother, who was eighty-five, and my grandpa, ninety-two years old. I have been hearing that life expectancy in Africa is low, but this shows the opposite, as most all my family members live above half a century. For centuries, many lies have been told about Africa, to keep Africans in doubt and under control.

These lies confirm the fact that history is full of lies; people become slaves when somebody else tells them their story. And Africa is one of the nations that had its story told by others.

Grandson, I blame the motherland, I blame the fake leaders that have been feeding of the blood of the innocent children. When I think about this continent, the one named the "black continent," even though my skin is brown like most Africans, we are just tired of the black color they gave us and assimilated it with hunger, poverty, war, and misery. From the Nile to the Congo going through the Zambezi, Africa, oh Africa, how wealthy are you? How rich are you? But your children are dying, they are slaves, they are illegal immigrants in other countries. Everybody feeds on you, but you never run dry; how blessed are you? How great are you? How abundant are you? How fruitful are you? Your children run across the sea to consume some of your tears, but they are seen as tyrants, thieves, monsters, and blacks.

Grandson, things are getting even worse for Africa. Well, we heard about the United States of Africa, it has been a century now. When we look back, it was even easier to create that United States of Africa. Nowadays, people look at the United States of America as a perfect image of what the United States of Africa would be. It is a good dream, but it will be hard for it to happen, as most countries are feeding on Africa. To start, Africans need to find a different name instead of United States of Africa, because there is only one USA, and that is the United States of America. Now we hear names like UNITED AFRICA, UNION OF AFRICAN STATES, AFRICAN STATES UNION, or just AFRICA. In fact, during my time in America, I learned that many Americans think that Africa is a country. It is true that they are ignorant, but sometimes I feel like it's a prophecy, even though if they find out what Africa will look like as a country, they will be shaken.

I'm not saying that Africa unified will solve all the issues that Africa is going through right now, but I think that if the leaders haven't made it happen, at least they have tried.

Many countries still need visas to go from one country to another, and they have been meeting for a common currency region by region, but no one has come out with something yet or reliable. Our lovely brave guide Gadafi, the leader of the Libyan revolution, was betray by his fellow African presidents, even though he was helping to craft the one and only Africa, with common currency that was supposed to be out by 2015. The African people are tired of this, and the motherland cannot tolerate that its children keep going through these wars and this terrorism that are supported by some people and governments of the West to keep us under control. We all know that nobody is going to come and develop Africa for Africans. How is it that fifty-four leaders cannot stand against their old colonizers and just tell them "we don't need you anymore." I think Africans must choose to be a colony or be totally free. I would have preferred to be a colony and enjoy having a French citizenship instead of being free by the book but just living as their lap dog. At this point, the leaders are confirming that they cannot do it; most of them are weak. They cannot be trusted anymore, because if we don't fight, it will never happen. So it is important that the young generation stand for Africa and unify it. The most advanced countries are the ones that install those leaders to serve them. Come on, where is your pride as presidents—we see that most of them were forgotten when they died or were cast out of power. A good leader should be able to die for his people and fight for them. There are only few Western countries that help Africa. We need to stand and say no to conditional help, because most of them come saying that they want to help but in fact they are just destroying and using all the resources. Honestly, with Africa United, we will not have groups like Boko Haram, Ansar Dine, wars in Central Africa, Congo...because we will have a strong army and we will crush any rebellion before it starts. And terrorists would never be a nightmare.

When Westerners go to Africa, they tell Africans that they are poor and they deserve better, and that keeps them thinking likewise, which means Africans will not do anything but sit and wait for their corrupt governments to bring change. The French education system is the worst education system inherited by Africans. All British colonized countries are doing far better than French ones, because the British education has helped them understand a way of life that is based on hard work rather than unrealistic pride. In fact, the French education system teaches students how to work in an office and talk nonsense or unnecessary debates, but in places like Africa, as well as many other nations, there are not enough government jobs for everyone to work in an office. Imagine if every American were to go to school to work a government job, it would be a mess; people in French-speaking nations, even those with master's and doctorates, end up at home or on the streets. Every nation and every people write their own history, but Western countries are acting like they want to help Africa write its history. Africa doesn't need help. Without Westerners around, Africa could have reached the level of development it is at now and even better. If Westerners were helping Africa, things would have been very different today. In fact, they keep dividing Africa like they did years ago to pull as much resources as possible. Countries like France will not survive without their hand in Africa. They have been the sponsors of wars and destabilizations in Africa, because without Africa, there would be no France. Former president of France Jacques Chirac acknowledged this when he said, "Without Africa, France would be a third-world country."

Africa needs partners, not charity advocates or bad faith nations that are just there to blindfold people and steal resources. Africa is full of brilliant and smart people; the diversity in resources is inestimable. Africa needs to stop playing games and stand up by dumping all the weak leaders. It is now or never, because if you don't start now it will never be. How can people think that Westerners are just there to help Africa? Every nation has its own problems, and Africans need to understand that when people come to them, they need Africa's help to sustain their economy and maintain their leadership in the world, so Grandson, you need to understand that we don't need them—they are the ones who need us. They always come with words like *education*, *health*, and *water*. All these are good things, right, but in fact that is colonization; they tell us what to do, when to do it, and how long to do it. By the way, which clean water are they talking about when some are dumping their industrial waste in Africa? Also, Ebola was in Congo for centuries and never killed even ten people at the same time, but after we heard that Africa is the fastest-growing economy, Ebola appeared thousands of miles from Congo and killed thousands of people in a short period, sending the African economy back to its knees. That made me remember one of the theories of my grandpa, which states that "HIV/AIDS was conceived to exterminate Africans and take their resources."

It is important for Africa to be united. My grandpa used to tell me that it is not very effective to pick up ashes with one hand. It may only be done with two hands. To unify Africa, a lot of sacrifices need to be made, and one of them is how current presidents will be willing to change their status from the most powerful to a humble governor of a state. There have never been clear propositions on how leaderships will be handled. Since some leaders have been in power for a few years and their countries have no term limits, it should be recommended that in the process of the United Africa, they can automatically become governors of their states and should be offered amnesty to run for as many terms as they wish. Afterward, regulations should be applied to any newcomer. But for all these recommendations, it is important to look at the education system that is more focused on Western governance. Africans are fortunate to have English, French, and Portuguese as languages. In fact, Africa should use the divisive system put together by colonizers to strengthen its unity. Since there are hundreds of languages, it is possible use them to easily communicate within the continent, as they will facilitate interactions between our people. Also, it should add lessons from Africa's education system about how important the unity of Africa is, going from kindergarten to the university.

Every kid needs to grow up knowing that his or her country, Africa, been torn apart and that his or her duty is to restore it. In recent years, a few organizations in African society have been fighting for better life conditions, but it is time to change the target, to widen the battle—it is time that all these organizations focus on the bigger goal of better life conditions: "The United Africa." The youth movements that have mounted resistance to presidents in Senegal, Burkina Faso, Congo, and Burundi need to create ties with all the youth of Africa and fight for the right cause, because "United, Africa may lead the world." Statistics have shown that Congo alone could feed Africa for centuries, yet the people in Congo remain among the poorest in the world.

Africa cannot continue to be the milk cow of Western countries. It is unbelievable that after almost sixty years of independence, they are unable to feed themselves, cure themselves, or even have a common currency that could boost the economy. Common currency should be the first priority—create the African money. At least, for the currency, it takes just to look at the example of the United States of America with the dollars, which in part makes America great. From North Dakota to Texas and from New York to California, the same dollars are spent without hesitation. China, with its yen, is also becoming more and more strong as it carries a big population and a wide territory; but Africa would be the ideal next superpower with a big population and more resources than any other country on earth. United, Africa will have the strongest economy, currency, and maybe military; it will surely be a strong ally to the United States in enforcing democracy and freedom to the rest of the world. Africa united will also improve road systems, railroads, and air traffic systems as the need for them will intensify and the future Federal Reserve should be able to finance any of these projects. In addition to that, Africa is a big market that no one can ignore. Africa could survive and even become better by itself.

This is a call for African youth to step into the battle and take back their continent. There are many friends in the West who would partner and assist Africa in this battle toward gaining full autonomy and unity. Grandson, hopefully a better future will be secure for you so that you will not have to go across the ocean for a better life...for the best will be there at home.

QUOTES

When I was growing up, snakes were the only things that made us unsafe, but today, everywhere I go, I do not trust the other person walking beside me. In fact, every day, I walk out of my house feeling like I'm a martyr because I do not know if I will make it back home safe.

—Nate Zop

We cannot deny that in every religion, there has been at a certain time some type of terrorism involved.

—Nate Zop

Every life matters and everyone who takes or tries to take a human life in the name of any ideology or religion is a terrorist and should be punished by the court of the law.

—Nate Zop

You can never win a war against terror as long as there are conditions in the world that make people desperate—poverty, disease, ignorance.

—Desmond Tutu

About the Author

Nate Zop is a US Army veteran. Holding a master's degree in security management, he has worked for the Department of Homeland Security, and his impressive experience with interreligious relations has been invaluable in the creation of this book.